# Mr. How Do You Do Sees Creation & You

Written By Kelly Johnson

Illustrated by Jan Hamilton

*Mr. How Do You Do* is a children's series featuring personified birds in whimsical stories that captivate children of all ages and help them grow in a vibrant relationship with Jesus.

Published by
Innovo Publishing LLC
www.innovopublishing.com
1-888-546-2111

Providing Full-Service Publishing Services for
Christian Authors, Artists and Organizations:
Books, eBooks, Audiobooks, Music & Film

MR. HOW DO YOU DO SEES CREATION & YOU


Library of Congress Catalog Card Number: 20159-56211
ISBN 13: 978-1-61314-321-6

Cover Design & Interior Layout by Innovo Publishing LLC
Cover Art & Illustrations by Jan Hamilton

Printed in the United States of America
U.S. Printing History
First Edition: August, 2016

# Dedication

This book is dedicated to a dear friend and exceptional artist.

At the outset of the Mr. How Do You Do Series, I had no idea who God would use to capture the whimsy and joy of the main character and his feathered friends. But God knew exactly who to task with this assignment and I believe gave us His best.

When Jan Hamilton picks up a paintbrush the canvas comes to life. Her humility precedes each stroke and that's precisely why the Creator can create such masterpieces through her. She's quick to give Creator God all the glory for her talent and even credits Him with guiding her paintbrush and waking her in the night with creative ideas and directives.

For Jan, artwork far surpasses creating on a canvas or page; artwork is expressing the Creator's love and magnificence to each person she meets. Thank you, Jan, for painting this world with His love!

Last night I looked up
in the galaxy . . .
thinking, How did this world
come to be?

The stars they filled
the nighttime sky.
The moon it hung
WAAAAAY Up high.

The
grass
beneath me
tickled my feet,
and its hair-like
strands were
far too
neat.

The lightning bugs
buzzed as they lit up the
night.
I think they knew who
created their
LIGHT.

The wise old owl made me think WHO had created me . . . had created you?

Surely, someone had designed every flower.

But I wondered WHO on earth had that power?

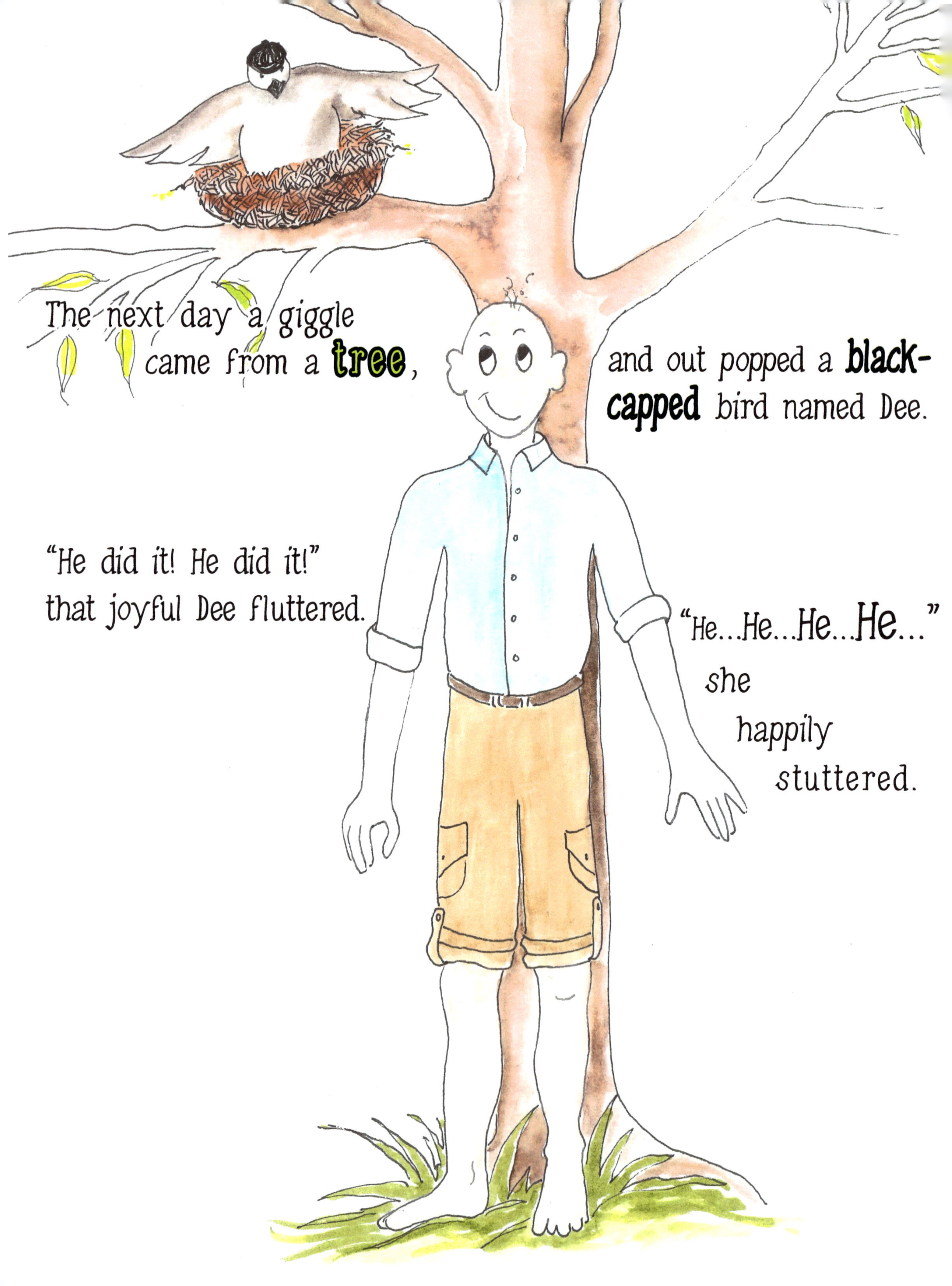

The next day a giggle came from a tree, and out popped a black-capped bird named Dee.

"He did it! He did it!" that joyful Dee fluttered.

"He...He...He...He..." she happily stuttered.

"Now what's that you say?" I greeted this guest.

Then back she came with
something **black** in her beak.

Her **heart** all a-flutter
Dee would heartily speak.

She dropped a tiny
black seed in my hand.

Then went on to tell me
of sea and of land.

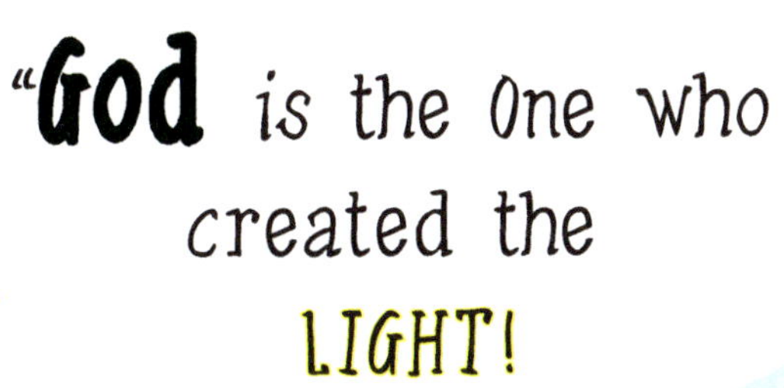


"God is the One who created the LIGHT!

He created the day!

He created the night!

He created the waters,
He created the sky.

He created the birds,
and He taught us to fly."

"He created every fish in the sea.
He created every plant, every tree."

"Do you see that **seed** in your hand?

Out of that, a million **forests** He planned."

"He's the best-est ever **Creator** He.
He created **you**. . . . He created **me**!

Oh! That's why I flutter
and that's why I sing.

My **heart** makes
me stutter,
especially in
spring."

"He wants you to find Him, He wants you to know.
Creation reminds us, so Come On . . . Let's Go!

let's take a hike . . .
look around you will see.

The **Creator** is speaking
both to you and to me."

They chased a **butterfly** for what seemed like hours.
And they studied its wings
as it flew through
the flowers.

Its wings they waved so
**colorful** and **bright**.
Why surely the Creator had
given it flight.

They grew a bit tired so they stopped for a rest.
Dee sat on his toes and said, "This is the best.

**Who** gave you fingers?
**Who** gave you toes?
Fashioned your eyes,
your ears,
and your nose?"

"Did you know Creator God knows each hair on your head?"
"He watches over you, even when you're in bed."

"Dee, this is AMAZING! I knew there was a Creator.
Not just a man but somebody greater.

God really did create
YOU and ME.

He speaks
through His Creation,
let's ask Him,
we'll see . . ."

# Prayer For Kids
# To Pray Out Loud

"**Dear Jesus,**

Thank You for creating me.

Thank You for birds, especially Dee.

Continue to show us and all our new friends

Creation is speaking and it never ends!"


**Did you know:** The stars twinkle saying, "Look at God above?"

**Did you know:** Showers sprinkle as they rain down His love?

And you, yes you, there reading this story . . .

**Did you know:** That God created YOU for His glory?

So shine, little friend, and look to God above...

He created YOU for great things; He created YOU in love.

Mr. How Do You Do tried to fill

the God-shaped hole in his heart

with many things,

but *soon discovered*

only **Jesus** could fill

that empty place.

Would you like to ask **Jesus** to fill your  too?
Simply ask Him:

"Dear Jesus,
forgive my sin
and fill my ♥. Because
of the ✝, I give
my life to You."

# Steps to help a child receive Jesus as Savior

Try to be in a quiet place with a prayerful attitude.

1. They should understand they are sinners in need of God's forgiveness (Romans 3:23).
2. They should ask for His forgiveness and confess (repent of) their sin (1 John 1:9).
3. They should understand that God loves them, Jesus paid the price for their sin on the cross, and He died and rose again (Roman 5:8).
4. They must invite Christ to come into their heart as Lord and Savior (Romans 10:9-10).

Help them understand and say this prayer (out loud).

Father, I am a sinner and need your forgiveness. I ask you to forgive me of all my sins in Jesus' name. I confess and turn from sinning and doing wrong, right now. I believe Jesus died for my sin and rose again. I thank Him for loving me and dying on the cross for me. Jesus, come into my heart, right now, and be my Lord and Savior. Fill me with Your Holy Spirit. I thank You, Lord, for hearing my prayer and coming into my heart and saving me as Your Word promises. I love You, Lord, and ask You to help me to live for You all the days of my life, in Jesus' name. Amen.

Remind your child often:

We are saved by grace through faith in Christ alone (Ephesians 2:8).

Have your child print their name in the space provided, then sign and date this page for a forever reminder of their life-changing decision.

I ________________________________________________ accepted Jesus into my heart as my Lord and Savior. On this day, I gave my life to Jesus.

_______________________________  
DATE

_______________________________  
SIGNATURE

# MORE MR. HOW DO YOU DO FUN

Visit mrhowdo.com for more offerings with the MR. HOW DO YOU DO series, including more books, plush toys, kits and FREE downloads worth $19.95!

16" HUGGABLE PLUSH

# AN IMPORTANT NOTE TO PARENTS

For grown-ups and children alike, inviting Jesus into our hearts and being "born again" spiritually is the most important decision in life. So we've provided additional **FREE RESOURCES ON OUR WEBSITE AT MRHOWDO.COM** to more fully discuss how to trust Jesus as your Savior and have a personal relationship with Him. These resources will help you talk with your child about sin and how to be forgiven and reconciled to God forever through our Savior - JESUS.

We also want you to know that although salvation (i.e., being born again spiritually and thus being reconciled with God for eternity) is a one-time event, Mr. How Do You Do will share his salvation experience at the end of each book in the series. That's because we want everyone who reads these books to know about Jesus and how to be saved.

# MEET THE AUTHOR & ILLUSTRATOR

**ABOUT THE AUTHOR:** Kelly Johnson is a lover of Jesus. She's convinced as children (of all ages) encounter His love and His character—in a relational way—their lives will be forever changed. Mr. How Do You Do is a whimsical, joy-filled teacher. Her prayer is that through his stories, many will learn invaluable life lessons and experience lavish love and boundless joy!  Kelly is a prayer warrior and frequent speaker. She is available in person or via Skype for readings, speaking engagements, book clubs, book signings, church events and women's events.  Write to:  Kelly@mrhowdo.com.

**ABOUT THE ILLUSTRATOR:** Jan Hamilton is grateful for the opportunity and gift of art the Lord has provided, allowing her to be a part of the Mr. How Do You Do series. "He is the author and finisher of our faith. Everything I am and have is a gift from Him."  Jan is a bible teacher and frequent speaker. She is available in person or via Skype for readings, speaking engagements, book clubs, book signings, church events and women's events.  Write to:  Jan@mrhowdo.com.

# Enjoy More Titles & Plush Toys From

## Innovo Catalog

Browse Innovo's Books, eBooks, Audiobooks, Music and Film.

**View Catalog**

## Henry's Life as a Tulip Bulb:

*Developing An Attitude of Gratitude*

**Book & Plush**

## David, Son of Jesse

*Growing Up Strong In the Lord*
*An Inspirational Story for Children*

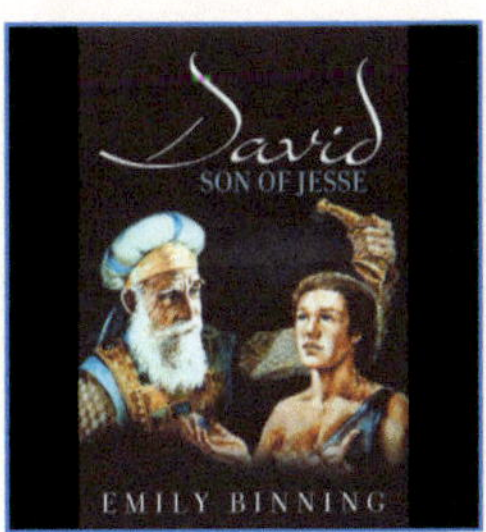

**Ages 10 & Up**

## Bully Trouble:

*Little Tommy Learns a Lesson*
*in Loving His Enemies*

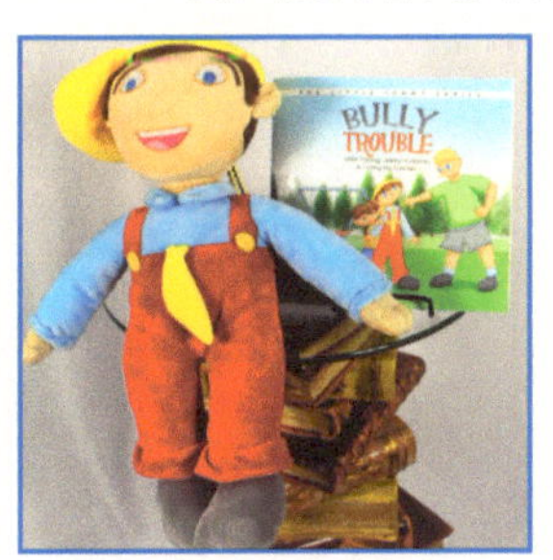

**Book & Plush**

# Writesie.com

### Custom Plush
### Animals, Figures & Pets

### Custom Books,
### eBooks & Audiobooks